▶ Decoding Strategies

Decoding B2
Workbook

Siegfried Engelmann • Linda Meyer • Linda Carnine
• Wesley Becker • Julie Eisele • Gary Johnson

SRA
McGraw-Hill
Columbus, Ohio

A Division of The **McGraw·Hill** *Companies*

SRA/McGraw-Hill

A Division of The McGraw·Hill Companies

2002 Imprint
Copyright © 1999 by SRA/McGraw-Hill.

Send all inquiries to:
SRA/McGraw-Hill
8787 Orion Place
Columbus, OH 43240-4027

Printed in the United States of America.

ISBN 0-02-674787-1

7 8 9 POH 04 03 02

1 Write the answers to these questions:
1. How many stink bugs lived in the garden? _____
2. What made the stink bugs proud? _____
3. What kind of contest were the bugs having? _____

_____

4. Name two animals that did not like what the stink bugs were doing.

_____

5. What did the smallest stink bug have on her back? _____
6. The smallest stink bug kept talking about how bad her stink was. What happened as

she kept talking? _____

2 Write these words without endings.
1. striped _____
2. jogged _____
3. stacker _____
4. rider _____
5. pinned _____
6. later _____
7. faster _____

3 Match the words and complete them.

skunks   br

being   ow

bright   skunks

stinker   er

low   ing

4 Write the 2nd sentence of Story 1.

_____

_____

LESSON 2

1 Write the 2 words that make up each word.

cannot = _____ + _____

herself = _____ + _____

understand = _____ + _____

anything = _____ + _____

boatload = _____ + _____

2 Write these words without endings.

1. picker _____

2. snoring _____

3. skipped _____

4. winked _____

5. slapping _____

6. baker _____

3 Write the answers to these questions:

1. How many bugs had already shown off their best stink? _____

2. Only two bugs were left. Who were they? _____

_____

3. Why did the biggest bug really go to the other side of the garden?

_____

_____

4. What did the little bug do after the biggest bug had run away?

_____

5. Who came to see what all the loud sounds were about? _____

6. Why did the little bug say she would never make a stink?

_____

4 Write the 1st sentence of Story 2.

_____

_____

1 Write the word **snail.** Make a line under **ai.** _____

Write the word **pouch.** Make a line over **ou.** _____

2 Write these words without endings.

1. shaved _____

2. stunned _____

3. sinking _____

4. later _____

5. thinking _____

6. batter _____

3 Write the answers to these questions:

1. What did Art look like when he was fifteen years old?

_____

2. Why didn't Art hang out with the other kids? _____

_____

3. What sport did Art try out for? _____

4. What did Art do at the pond? _____

5. In which class did Patty sit in front of Art? _____

6. What did Art show the class? _____

7. Who told Art that he gave a very good talk? _____

8. What did Art give Patty? _____

9. Who made fun of Art after Patty left? _____

4 Write the 2 words that make up each word.

greenhouse = _____ + _____

homework = _____ + _____

himself = _____ + _____

doorway = _____ + _____

inside = _____ + _____

1 Write **1, 2,** or **3** in front of each sentence to show when these things happened in the story. Then write the sentences in the blanks.

_____ **One day Art stopped at the lot to watch the baseball team.**

_____ **Art skipped a stone all the way to the other side of the pond.**

_____ **Art said that he could throw the ball faster than the other pitcher.**

1. _____

_____

2. _____

_____

3. _____

_____

2 Write these words without endings.

1. louder   _____   5. striped   _____

2. deeply   _____   6. clearly   _____

3. staring   _____   7. boating   _____

4. reader   _____   8. finest   _____

3 Write the answers to these questions:

1. Why didn't Art ever tell Patty that he wanted her to be his girl friend?

_____

_____

2. Who was Patty's boy friend? _____

3. What did Bart think about the pitcher?

_____

4. What did everybody do when Art said that he could throw the ball faster than the pitcher?

_____

1 Write the name of the person each sentence tells about.

              Art   **catcher**   **coach**

1. This person's arm went back and then came forward like a whip. _____

2. This person was on his seat. _____

3. This person was blowing on his hand. _____

4. This person said he had never seen anybody throw a ball that hard. _____

5. This person had a gift to become a fine pitcher. _____

6. This person didn't sleep well because he kept thinking about pitching. _____

7. This person said, "When I see what you can't do, I'll know what we have to work on." _____

8. This person stuffed a big rag into his mitt. _____

2 Write these words without endings.

1. dearly   _____   5. waiter   _____

2. floated   _____   6. liked   _____

3. smiled   _____   7. loaded   _____

4. sounding   _____   8. hearing   _____

3 Write the 2 words that make up each word.

greenhouse = _____ + _____

everybody = _____ + _____

without = _____ + _____

football = _____ + _____

motorcycle = _____ + _____

4 Write the 1st sentence of Story 5.

_____

1 Read the sentences and answer the questions.
Art worked out with the baseball team after school.
After three weeks, the team had its first game.

1. Who did Art work out with? _____

2. When did the team work out? _____

3. What happened after the team worked out for three weeks?

_____

2 Write the answers to these questions:

1. Why did the catcher stuff a rag into his mitt?

_____

2. Who showed Art how to throw a curve ball? _____

3. Why did the coach put in different catchers to work with Art?

_____

_____

4. What team did Art's team play first? _____

5. How many times had Art's school beaten West High before? _____

6. What things was Art telling himself as he pitched to the first batter?

_____

3 The words in the first column have endings. Write the same words without endings in the second column.

batter _____

beaten _____

glared _____

lonely _____

staring _____

4 Write the 3rd sentence of Story 6.

_____

_____

1 Write **1, 2,** or **3** in front of each sentence to show when these things happened in the story. Then write the sentences in the blanks.

_____ **The catcher tossed the ball to Art, and Art dropped it.**

_____ **The coach for the Tigers asked Art to pitch the first inning of the game.**

_____ **Art pitched to some big league players before the game.**

1. _____

_____

2. _____

_____

3. _____

_____

2 Write the answers to these questions:

1. A player told Art to throw fast balls. What did he think the batters would do to Art's

fast balls? _____

_____

2. How far did James Hunt hit the ball? _____

3. When Art started to pitch the first inning of the game, he became afraid. What did he start to think about?

_____

3 The words in the first column have endings. Write the same words without endings in the second column.

tired _____

whipped _____

jailer _____

shaking _____

winner _____

1 Read the sentence and answer the questions.
As Art stood on the pitcher's mound, his hands felt cold.

1. What happened as Art stood on the pitching mound?

_____

2. Where was Art? _____

3. When did Art's hands feel cold?

_____

2 Write the name of the person each sentence tells about.

Art   nurse   catcher

1. This person yelled, "Just zip it right in here," and pounded his fist into his mitt.   _____

2. There was a story about this person's pitching in the paper.   _____

3. This person did not want the other kids to think that he was afraid to be in a fast car.   _____

4. This person said, "You are lucky to be alive."   _____

5. This person was in a very bad crash.   _____

3 Write the 2 words that make up each word.

handshake   =   _____   +   _____

everything   =   _____   +   _____

nothing   =   _____   +   _____

football   =   _____   +   _____

yourself   =   _____   +   _____

4 Match the words and complete them.

flight	ex
exhibition	sand
thousand	hos
dollars	fl
hospital	ars

1 Write the answers to these questions:

1. What had happened to Art's arm? _____

2. What did the doctor tell Art that made him start to sob? _____
_____

3. Whom did Art see when he was in the hospital?
_____

4. Name some people Art would not see when he was in the hospital. _____
_____

5. After Art went home from the hospital, what did he do for the next week?
_____

6. How did Art's arm feel? _____
7. How did the doctor get the cast off Art's arm?
_____

2 The words in the first column have endings. Write the same words without endings in the second column.

closer   _____

hardest   _____

jogged   _____

leaving   _____

speaker   _____

3 Match the words and complete them.

falling   lea

voice   se

league   v

should   ing

nurse   ld

4 Write the 3rd sentence of Story 11.

_____

1 Write **1**, **2**, or **3** in front of each sentence to show when these things happened in the story. Then write the sentences in the blanks.

_____ **Everybody tried to be friends with Art.**

_____ **Patty asked Art to try skipping stones.**

_____ **Patty told Art that he should tell himself that he could pitch again.**

1. _____

   _____

2. _____

   _____

3. _____

   _____

2 Write the answers to these questions:

1. How many kids told Art that they were sorry?

   _____

2. How did Art feel about people saying that they were sorry?

   _____

3. How strong was Art's arm after a year passed?

   _____

4. One day Art was near the pond when he saw Patty. What was Patty doing?

   _____

3 The words in the first column have endings. Write the same words without endings in the second column.

broken   _____

driver   _____

hardly   _____

winner   _____

strapped   _____

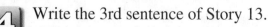

1 Write the words.

every + body = _____

hand + shake = _____

cheer + leader = _____

some + where = _____

steam + ship = _____

2 Write the name of the person each sentence tells about.

Patty   Art

1. This person didn't want to skip stones. _____

2. This person felt ashamed. _____

3. This person wanted to have a stone-skipping contest. _____

4. The first time this person tried to skip a stone, it didn't skip one time. _____

5. This person said, "You just have to start being brave." _____

6. This person had liked being a show-off. _____

7. This person began to work, exercise, and skip stones. _____

3 Match the words and complete them.

heavy	nds
exercise	ag
friends	ce
again	vy
once	ex

4 Write the 3rd sentence of Story 13.

_____

1 Read the sentence and answer the questions.
In the first game, Art's brains were tested.

1. Whose brains were tested? _____

2. When were they tested? _____

3. What happened in the first game?

_____

2 Write the answers to these questions:

1. When Art went out for baseball, what did the boys on the team tell him to do?

_____

2. What were some of the things that the coach told Art that Art could still do well?

_____

3. The coach told Art that now he was going to have to win games by using something. What was he going to have to use?

_____

4. What did the catcher tell Art? _____

_____

5. What is Art doing today? _____

6. Who is Art's wife and biggest fan? _____

3 The words in the first column have endings. Write the same words without endings in the second column.

smartest _____

moped _____

nearly _____

rubbed _____

timing _____

4 Write the word **further.** Make a box around **ur.** 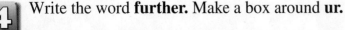 _____

Write the word **halfway.** Make a line over **half.** _____

1 Write the answers to these questions:

1. Where did the president tell the cab driver to take them?

_____

2. The president went up to a woman. What did he ask her?

_____

3. What did the president tell the woman that he was?

_____

4. What did the president tell the woman he would do if she didn't have a pass?

_____

5. How was the woman trying to bribe the president? _____

_____

6. How much did the president tell the woman that the pass would cost?

_____

7. How did the president show that the woman had a pass?

_____

8. How much money did the president give the cab driver?

_____

2 The words in the first column have endings. Write the same words without endings in the second column.

filed _____

gripped _____

player _____

cleanly _____

moping _____

3 Write the word **catch.** Make a line under **tch.** _____

Write the word **coach.** Make a box around **oa.** _____

1 Write the answers to these questions:

1. Where did the president tell the con man they were going?

_____

2. The president asked the woman at the desk for a list. What was on that list? _____

_____

3. What did the president say his assistant's name was?

_____

4. What did the president say his name was? _____

5. The president said that the woman could fix his name with three strokes of the pen. What

would she write? _____

6. What did the president say that he still needed for his trip to Japan?

_____

2 The words in the first column have endings. Write the same words without endings in the second column.

taking _____

slowly _____

pined _____

pinned _____

robber _____

3 Match the words and complete them.

batch • • take

mistake • • set

assistant • • b

foolish • • assist

upset • • ish

4 Write the 2nd sentence of Story 16.

_____

_____

1 Look at the picture and do the items.

1. Make the letter **C** on the con man.

2. Make the letter **R** on the ramp.

3. Make the letter **B** on the bags.

4. Make a **P** on the person who stopped the con man.

5. Write the words the con man said. _____

2 Write the answers to these questions:

1. Where had the president told the man with the cart to take the bags?

   _____

2. The con man was getting ready to split. Who stopped him?

   _____

3 Write the 2 words that make up each word.

halfway	=	_____	+	_____
everyone	=	_____	+	_____
outside	=	_____	+	_____
downhill	=	_____	+	_____
paintbrush	=	_____	+	_____

4 Write the word **thirst.** Make a box around **ir.**   _____

Write the word **quickly.** Make a box around **quick.**   _____

1 Read the sentence and answer the questions.

The tall man, who was almost taken to Happy Hollow Rest Home, was the victim of a plot.

1. Who was almost taken to Happy Hollow Rest Home? _____

2. Where was the tall man almost taken?

_____

2 Write the name of the person each sentence tells about.

president   Robert Fredrick   cop

1. This person found out that the con man was trying to steal his bags.   _____

2. This person said that the tall man was an impostor.   _____

3. This person asked the tall man for his identification.   _____

4. This person grabbed somebody's wallet.   _____

5. This person gave a blast on his whistle.   _____

6. This person was the victim of a plot.   _____

3 Write the words.

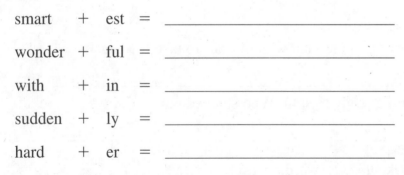

smart   +   est   =   _____

wonder   +   ful   =   _____

with   +   in   =   _____

sudden   +   ly   =   _____

hard   +   er   =   _____

4 The words in the first column have endings. Write the same words without endings in the second column.

pitcher   _____

proudly   _____

grabbed   _____

taken   _____

talking   _____

1 Write **1, 2,** or **3** in front of each sentence to show when these things happened in the story. Then write the sentences in the blanks.

_____ **The cop gave the tall man his wallet.**

_____ **The president told the con man why he told the truth.**

_____ **The president told the cops the truth about everything.**

1. _____

_____

2. _____

_____

3. _____

_____

2 Write the answers to these questions:

1. The president told the cops about how he had conned a lot of people. What had he conned

the hotel out of? _____

2. What had the president conned the rich woman out of? _____

3. What had the president conned the woman at the steamship line out of?

_____

4. What was the president trying to con the tall man out of? _____

5. Where did the cop say that the president and the con man should go?

_____

6. Why did the president say that he told the truth?

_____

3 The words in the first column have endings. Write the same words without endings in the second column.

faking   _____

quickly   _____

stared   _____

started   _____

conned   _____

LESSON 20

1 Write the answers to these questions:

1. Where does this story happen? _____

2. How old was Hurn? _____

3. How are the ears of puppy wolves different from the ears of adult wolves?

_____

_____

_____

4. Hurn saw the outline of a big cat. How big was the cat?

_____

5. What did the big cat and Hurn's mother do? _____

6. Who ran from the cave? _____

7. After the fight, what did Hurn's mother do to her puppies?

_____

_____

8. When Hurn woke up the next morning, what had happened to his mother?

_____

2 The words in the first column have endings. Write the same words without endings in the second column.

grabbed _____

nosed _____

suddenly _____

smiling _____

snapping _____

Write the word **delight.** Make a box around **light.** _____

Write the word **burn.** Make a line over **ur.** _____

1 Read the sentence and answer the questions.

If Hurn's mother had not scared the big cat from the cave, the big cat would have killed Hurn and Surt.

1. Who scared the big cat? _____

2. What would have happened if Hurn's mother had not scared the big cat? _____

_____

2 Look at the picture and do the items.

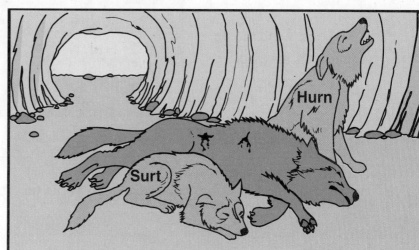

1. Make a **C** on the mouth of the cave.
2. Make a **W** on a wound that Hurn's mother suffered.
3. Make an **M** on Hurn's mother.
4. What is Hurn doing in the picture? _____
5. What is Surt doing in the picture? _____

3 Write the answers to these questions:

1. What happened to Hurn's mother? _____

2. What did Hurn and Surt do most of the day? _____

_____

3. Name some things Hurn and Surt would have done if their mother had not died.

_____

4 Write the 2 words that make up each word.

paintbrush = _____ + _____

anything = _____ + _____

homesick = _____ + _____

without = _____ + _____

1 Look at the picture and do the items.

1. Make an **H** on Hurn.
2. Make an **S** on Surt.
3. Make a **V** on Vern.
4. Make an **X** on the thing that Vern gave Surt.
5. Write what the other two men said.

2 The words in the first column have endings. Write the same words without endings in the second column.

scared   _____

cooking   _____

piped   _____

snapped   _____

smiling   _____

3 Match the words and complete them.

fern	ch
almost	to
poach	f
toward	gry
hungry	most

4 Write the 2nd sentence of Story 22.

_____

1 Write the name of the wolf each sentence tells about.

        Hurn   **Surt**

1. This wolf ate a chunk of meat. _____

2. This wolf burned a leg in the fire. _____

3. This wolf watched from behind a fern. _____

4. This wolf's mouth watered as the hunters ate. _____

5. This wolf wanted to start howling. _____

6. This wolf walked over to Vern and sat down next to him. _____

2 Write the answers to these questions:

1. Describe the night sky. _____

_____

2. What sounds came from the forest and the stream? _____

_____

3. What two things did Surt want at the end of this story?

_____

3 Write the words.

    walk + ing   = _____

    power + ful   = _____

    play + er   = _____

    quick + ly   = _____

    over + sight = _____

4 Match the words and complete them.

crouched	er
water	or
friends	ds
sparks	cr
orange	ks

 Look at the picture and do the items.

1. Write **Hurn** under the picture of Hurn.
2. Write **Surt** under the picture of Surt.
3. Write **Vern** over the picture of Vern.
4. Write **Bert** over the picture of Bert.

2 Write the answers to these questions:

1. Something told Hurn that Surt was no longer his sister. What was going to happen

to Surt? _____

_____

2. How did Hurn feel after leaving Surt and the hunters?

_____

3. What did Hurn try to catch the next morning? _____

4. What happened to Hurn when he tried to catch the animal?

_____

 Write the word **purple.** Make a line over **ur.** _____

Write the word **walking.** Make a box around **walk.** _____

1 Read the sentence and answer the questions.
When the tan wolf began to leave, Hurn jumped up, ran after her, and bit her back leg.

1. Who started to leave? _____

2. When did Hurn jump up? _____

_____

3. What did Hurn do after he ran after the tan wolf?

_____

2 Write the answers to these questions:

1. How many pups had the tan wolf given birth to? _____

2. How many of the pups were still alive? _____

3. What did Hurn do when the tan wolf came close to him? _____

_____

4. The tan wolf nipped Hurn and he rolled over on his back. What did that show the

   tan wolf? _____

_____

3 The words in the first column have endings. Write the same words without endings in the second column.

chasing ——————————————

patting ——————————————

scared ——————————————

stiffly ——————————————

wagged ——————————————

4 Write the 2nd sentence of Story 25.

_____

_____

LESSON 26

1 Look at the picture and do the items.

1. Make a box around the tan wolf and her pup.
2. Write **Hurn** on Hurn.
3. Write **brown wolf** next to the brown wolf.
4. Color the black wolf **black.**

2 Write the answers to these questions:

1. What did the tan wolf do to the brown wolf when she heard Hurn howl?

   _____

2. When the tan wolf stood next to Hurn and stared at the other wolves, she was telling them something. What was that? _____

3. How long had Hurn lived with the tan wolf? _____

4. How did Hurn feel about the tan wolf? _____

3 Write the words.

crouch + ed = _____

it + self = _____

talk + ing = _____

bull + frog = _____

butter + flies = _____

1 Write **1, 2,** or **3** in front of each sentence to show when these things happened in the story. Then write the sentences in the blanks.

_____ **The black wolf let Hurn stay in the hollow.**

_____ **The tan wolf crouched down and growled at Hurn.**

_____ **Hurn was hurt, and he didn't know what to do.**

1. _____

   _____

2. _____

   _____

3. _____

   _____

2 Write the answers to these questions:

1. Name some of the things that Hurn had hunted.

   _____

2. Why did the tan wolf growl at Hurn when he came back from hunting?

   _____

3. How did Hurn show the black wolf that the black wolf was the boss?

   _____

4. As Hurn got older, what happened to his fur?

   _____

5. Hurn looked a lot like the black wolf. How were the two wolves different?

   _____

3 The words in the first column have endings. Write the same words without endings in the second column.

darker   _____

hopped   _____

tugging   _____

stiffly   _____

wiped   _____

1 Look at the picture and do the items.

1. Make a box around the wolf that did not fight.
2. Make an **S** on the wolf that was smarter.
3. Make an **F** on the wolf that was faster.
4. Circle the wolf that wins all the fights.
5. Make a line under the wolf that became the leader of the new pack.

2 Write the answers to these questions:

1. While the other wolves were being fooled, what did the black wolf do?

_____

2. Why would some of the wolves have to leave the pack?

_____

3. What did the black wolf do after the wolves had eaten the fox?

_____

4. How many wolves left the pack? _____

5. Who was the boss of these wolves? _____

3 Write the 2 words that make up each word.

daytime	=	_____	+ _____
sunlight	=	_____	+ _____
hilltop	=	_____	+ _____
throughout	=	_____	+ _____
freeway	=	_____	+ _____

1 Read the sentence and answer the questions.

As Hurn and the other wolves slowly walked down the side of the mountain, a big black bear came out of its den.

1. Where were Hurn and the other wolves walking?

   _____

2. How were they walking? _____

3. What came out of its den? _____

2 Write the name of the animal each sentence tells about.

        Hurn   **black bear**   **black wolf**

1. This animal had been sleeping nearly all winter. _____

2. This animal didn't want to run away any more. _____

3. This animal rubbed its tender nose and walked
   back up the side of the mountain. _____

4. This animal had a fight and left the pack. _____

5. This animal led the pack for nine years. _____

6. This animal found a wolf pup and saved her. _____

3 The words in the first column have endings. Write the same words without endings in the second column.

    badly   _____

    quicker   _____

    stirring   _____

    nipped   _____

    striped   _____

4 Write the 3rd sentence of Story 29.

_____

_____

LESSON 30

1 Look at the picture and do the items.

1. Who is talking in this picture? _____

2. Who is thinking in this picture? _____
3. Write **Carl** on the picture of Carl.
4. Write a **W** on the woman who ran the boarding house.
5. Make a **B** on Berta.

2 Write the answers to these questions:

1. Where did Irma and three of the women who lived in the boarding house work?

   _____

2. What would the people who lived in the house do after dinner?

   _____

3. What would Irma do first after dinner? _____

4. What did Irma like to do most of all? _____
5. What had Irma been working on for over a year?

   _____

3 Match the words and complete them.

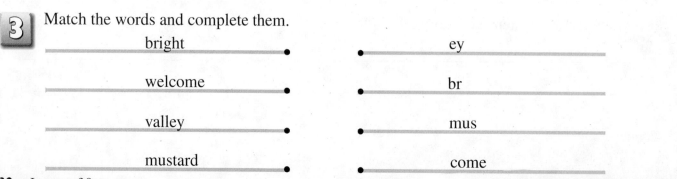

bright •   • ey

welcome •   • br

valley •   • mus

mustard •   • come

1 Look at the picture and do the items.

1. Which man is talking in the picture? _____
2. Part of what he said is missing. Write the missing words in the blank.

3. Which woman is talking? _____
4. Where is she going? _____
5. Part of what she said is missing. Write the missing word in the blank.

2 Write the answers to these questions:

1. How long had the paint been drying in the jars? _____

2. What was the paint in the last jar like? _____
3. How did Irma test how hard the paint in the last jar was?

   _____

4. Irma went upstairs to get pretzels for Herman. Where did she leave the nail?

   _____

5. What couldn't Irma find when she went back to her lab? _____

6. What had happened to the nail? _____

3 Write the words.

     wash + er   = _____

     what + ever = _____

     power + ful = _____

     want + ed   = _____

1 Look at the picture and do the items.

1. Write the name of each person on the picture of that person.

Herman   Carl   Fern   Berta   Irma

2. Part of what people are saying is missing. Write the missing words in the blanks.

3. What is Fern doing in the picture? _____

2 Write the name of the person each sentence tells about.

Irma   Berta   Carl   Fern

1. This person said, "You wanted a hand? Here it is."   _____

2. This person took a dive out the window.   _____

3. This person ran out the door as fast as a track star.   _____

4. This person sat down on the floor and laughed.   _____

5. This person fainted three times.   _____

6. This person took a shower and put on clean clothes.   _____

3 Write the 2 words that make up each word.

itself   = _____   +   _____

upstairs   = _____   +   _____

someday   = _____   +   _____

bullfrog   = _____   +   _____

whatever   = _____   +   _____

1 Look at the picture and do the items.

1. Who is person A? _____

2. What is person A saying? _____

   _____

3. Who is person B? _____

4. What is person B saying? _____

   _____

2 Write the answers to these questions:

1. When Carl came in the front door, what was he carrying? _____

2. There was a knock at the door. Who was at the door? _____

3. Why did the cops think that Herman had flipped? _____

   _____

4. What did Herman stare at when he sat on the couch? _____

3 The words in the first column have endings. Write the same words without endings in the second column.

baked   _____

friendly   _____

smiling   _____

smarter   _____

shrugged   _____

1 Write the answers to these questions:

1. Irma made up her mind about two things. What were they?

_____

_____

_____

2. For the next three or four days after Irma had scared the boarders, how did they act?

_____

_____

3. How much paint did Irma fix? _____

4. What did Irma do with most of the paint?

_____

5. Irma filled three broiling pans with the rest of the paint. Where did she hide the pans

of paint? _____

_____

2 The words in the first column have endings. Write the same words without endings in the second column.

closed _____

flipped _____

harden _____

really _____

careful _____

3 Match the words and complete them.

movie   •   • ck

knock   •   • al

normal   •   • pl

stomped   •   • ie

place   •   • st

1 Write **1, 2,** or **3** in front of each sentence to show when these things happened in the story. Then write the sentences in the blanks.

_____ **Irma slipped Carl's keys into Herman's back pocket.**

_____ **Irma rubbed the invisible paint on every part of her.**

_____ **Irma dropped a chunk of ice down the back of Berta's dress.**

1. _____

_____

2. _____

_____

3. _____

_____

2 Write the answers to these questions:

1. Who did Berta think dropped the ice down her back? _____

2. What did Herman think Carl had done?

_____

3. Why couldn't Carl leave the house? _____

_____

4. What were the boarders doing at the end of this story?

_____

5. What was Irma doing at the end of this story? _____

6. Who had the keys? _____

3 Write the words.

board + er = _____

base + ment = _____

mean + est = _____

pocket + book = _____

stiff + ly = _____

1 Look at the picture and do the items.

YOU DON'T HAVE ANY IDEA, DO YOU? YOU DIDN'T TAKE THEM FROM MY COAT, DID YOU? YOU DIDN'T SWIPE THEM, DID YOU?

NO, I DIDN'T.

1. Write **Carl** on Carl.
2. Write **Herman** on Herman.
3. Make an **X** on the picture of the person who had a tooth knocked out.
4. What are Carl and Herman arguing about? _____

2 Read this sentence and answer the questions.
Carl was yelling because he couldn't find his keys.

1. Who was yelling? _____
2. Why was he yelling? _____
3. What couldn't he find? _____

3 Write the 2 words that make up each word.

bedroom = _____ + _____

downstairs = _____ + _____

nowhere = _____ + _____

without = _____ + _____

somehow = _____ + _____

4 Write the 3rd sentence of Story 38.

_____

_____

1 Write the name of the person each sentence tells about.

Irma   Herman   Berta   Fern

1. This person complained about going to the dentist. _____

2. This person loaned somebody money to pay the dentist bill. _____

3. This person was asleep in the living room chair. _____

4. This person looked as if she had two big holes in her head. _____

5. This person was the first person to faint. _____

6. This person fainted next. _____

7. This person had two teeth missing. _____

8. This person had one black eye. _____

2 Write the 2 words that make up each word.

bathroom = _____ + _____

rainbow   = _____ + _____

inside   = _____ + _____

butterflies = _____ + _____

sometimes = _____ + _____

3 Match the words and complete them.

circle	et
few	fr
quiet	w
front	cle
listen	li

4 Write the word **trailers.** Circle **ai.** _____

Write the word **bankers.** Make a box around **bank.** _____

1 Look at the picture and do the items.

1. Make an **X** on the thing everyone is looking at.
2. Make two black eyes on Carl.
3. Who is leaving the room? _____
4. What is he getting ready to do? _____
5. Part of what Irma said is missing. Write the missing word.

2 Write the answers to these questions:

1. Who went to the eye doctor? _____
2. Where did Fern go for a rest? _____
3. Why didn't Herman talk much? _____
   _____
4. Why did Irma feel good at the end of this story?
   _____

3 The words in the first column have endings. Write the same words without endings in the second column.

broken   _____

loudly   _____

poked   _____

biggest   _____

rubbing   _____

1 Write the answers to these questions:

1. Name three kinds of people who would love Irma's invisible paint.
_____

2. Name three kinds of people who would hate Irma's invisible paint.
_____

3. One day Irma made up her mind about the paint. Whom would she tell about the paint?
_____

4. Who left late in the summer? _____

5. What name does Irma have as a magician?
_____

6. What is the trick that people come from all over to see?
_____

7. Who is Irma's assistant? _____

8. Why have other magicians offered Irma thousands of dollars?
_____
_____

2 The words in the first column have endings. Write the same words without endings in the second column.

shrugged _____

trailer _____

checked _____

stared _____

joking _____

3 Write the word **price.** Make a line over **ce.** _____

Write the word **billboard.** Circle **bill.** _____

1 Look at the picture and do the items.

1. Who is person A?

   _____

2. Who is person B?

   _____

3. Part of what person B said is missing. Write the missing word in the blank.

4. Who is person C?

   _____

5. Part of what person C said is missing. Write the missing word in the blank.

2 Write **1, 2,** or **3** in front of each sentence to show when these things happened in the story. Then write the sentences in the blanks.

_____ **The boys and girls listened to Old Salt tell about his days as a first officer on cargo ships.**

_____ **The boys and girls began to make fun of Old Salt.**

_____ **Tony asked Salt what was in the trunk.**

1. _____

   _____

2. _____

   _____

3. _____

   _____

3 The words in the first column have endings. Write the same words without endings in the second column.

   certainly   _____

   griping   _____

   manned   _____

   filed   _____

1 Look at the picture and do the items.

1. Who is holding the map in the picture?

_____

2. Part of what one person said is missing. Write the missing words in the blanks.

3. Make an **X** on the person who was holding the letters before they fell on the floor.

4. Make a **Y** on the person who grabbed the letters and broke the string that bound them.

2 Write the answers to these questions:

1. When did Tony and Rosa go back to Old Salt's place?

_____

2. Why did Old Salt think Tony and Rosa came to his house?

_____

3. Name some of the things that were in the trunk. _____

_____

4. Old Salt didn't want Rosa to look at some things. What were they?

_____

5. What did Tony find that was in with one of the letters?

_____

6. What did Old Salt have to do before he could become rich?

_____

3 Write the words.

late + ly = _____

shot + gun = _____

to + night = _____

trail + er = _____

care + ful = _____

1 Use the code in this story (on page 91) to figure out this secret message.

19	19		6	15	9	12
☐	☐		☐	☐	☐	☐

18	15	19	5		9	19	12	1	14	4
☐	☐	☐	☐		☐	☐	☐	☐	☐	☐

2 Read the sentence and answer the questions.
Tony and the others worked on the code for an hour.

1. Who worked on the code? _____

2. What did Tony and the others do? _____

3. How long did Tony and the others work on the code? _____

3 The words in the first column have endings. Write the same words without endings in the second column.

shrugged _____

rested _____

robber _____

filing _____

noting _____

4 Match the words and complete them.

treasure	k
mumble	be
break	le
bridge	tr
because	ge

5 Write the 2nd sentence of Story 44.

_____

_____

1   This is part of the map that Rosa, Tony, and Old Salt found.

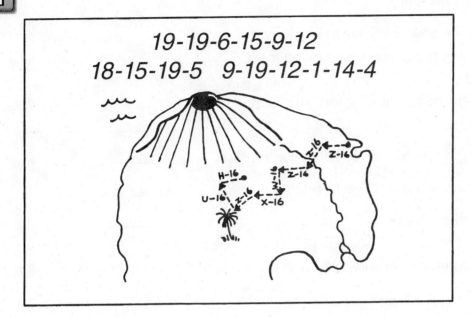

19-19-6-15-9-12
18-15-19-5 9-19-12-1-14-4

1. If you were at the tree on the map, how many more paces would you have to take to find

   the treasure? _____

2. What does it say at the top of the map? _____

3. Name some things you would see on Rose Island. _____

   _____

4. Make a **V** on the volcano.

5. Make a **C** on the cove where the captain landed.

2   The words in the first column have endings. Write the same words without endings in the second column.

     sticking   _____

     maker   _____

     robbed   _____

     noted   _____

     gripping   _____

3   Write the word **poison.** Circle **oi.**   _____

     Write the word **glasses.** Make a line under **glass.**   _____

LESSON 46

1 Write the name of the person each sentence tells about.

        Tony   **Old Salt**

1. This person said, "Not a word of this to anybody."   _____
2. This person was going to see about getting on a
    ship to Rose Island.   _____
3. This person sat on his bed for a long time, thinking
    about the treasure.   _____
4. This person wanted to tell everybody about the treasure.   _____
5. This person had a dream about a chest of gold.   _____
6. This person was boiling mad.   _____

2 The words in the first column have endings. Write the same words without endings in the second column.

weighed   _____

patted   _____

cones   _____

coping   _____

conning   _____

3 Write the words.

your   +   self   =   _____

boil   +   ed   =   _____

any   +   body   =   _____

quick   +   est   =   _____

down   +   stairs   =   _____

4 Write the 1st sentence of Story 46.

_____

_____

 Look at the picture and do the items.

1. Make an **X** on the person who found out about a vacation ship that was leaving for the South Pacific.

2. Part of what two people said is missing. Write the names of those persons.

_____

3. Write the missing words in the blanks.

Write the answers to these questions:

1. Why was Salt mad when Tony got to Salt's place? _____

_____

2. What did Salt tell Tony to do when he wanted to talk about the gold?

_____

3. What kind of ship was leaving for the South Pacific?

_____

4. How far would the ship go? _____

5. What did Tony and Rosa want to do? _____

Match the words and complete them.

knew   •   •   er _____

cheek   •   •   ch _____

nation   •   •   na _____

broiler   •   •   ew _____

LESSON 48

1 Write **1, 2,** or **3** in front of each sentence to show when these things happened in the story. Then write the sentences in the blanks.

_____ **Tony took a shower and changed into a clean outfit.**

_____ **Tony worked for four hours in the furnace room.**

_____ **Rosa and Tony talked their parents into letting them go on the trip to the South Pacific.**

1. _____

_____

2. _____

_____

3. _____

_____

2 Write the answers to these questions:

1. What job did Rosa get on the ship? _____

2. What job did Tony get on the ship?

_____

3. Name some tools that Salt took with him. _____

_____

4. Why did Tony get sick? _____

5. What was Salt's job on the ship? _____

_____

3 The words in the first column have endings. Write the same words without endings in the second column.

topped _____

fatter _____

hired _____

robbing _____

talking _____

1 Look at the picture and do the items.

Speech bubble (left): FOR YOU, I'LL LET YOU HAVE IT FOR _____ A DAY.

Speech bubble (right): THIS WOMAN THINKS SHE'S DEALING WITH A PACK OF RICH SUCKERS.

1. Draw a line from each person who is talking to the words that person is saying.
2. This picture took place on _____ Island.
3. Part of what one person said is missing. Write the missing words in the blank.

2 Write the answers to these questions:

1. Why did Tony think that he had the best job of all?

   _____

2. How long did it take the ship to reach Wake Island? _____
3. What kind of boat did Tony want? _____
4. What kind of boat did Salt want?

   _____

5. How much did the woman first ask for renting the boat?

   _____

6. For how much did the woman finally rent the boat?

   _____

3 Write the 2 words that make up each word.

afternoon	=	_____	+	_____
spotlight	=	_____	+	_____
whenever	=	_____	+	_____
nearby	=	_____	+	_____

LESSON 50

1 Write the answers to these questions:

1. Name some things that were on the beach at Wake Island.

_____

2. What did Salt pack in the boat?

_____

3. How had the sea changed by noon? _____

_____

4. Who was getting sick on the boat? _____

5. What kind of food did Salt pack for them to eat? _____

2 Read this sentence and answer the questions.

Every time the boat reached the top of a green swell, Tony could see the islands off to one side.

1. When could Tony see the islands? _____

_____

2. What color were the swells? _____

3. What could Tony see? _____

4. Who could see the islands? _____

3 The words in the first column have endings. Write the same words without endings in the second column.

slapped —————————————

biting —————————————

wanted —————————————

mopping —————————————

hidden —————————————

4 Use the code in Story 44 (on page 91) to figure out this secret message.

20	8	5	25		23	9	12	12
☐	☐	☐	☐		☐	☐	☐	☐

6	9	14	4		19	9	12	22	5	18
☐	☐	☐	☐		☐	☐	☐	☐	☐	☐

1 Look at the picture and do the items.

1. This picture took place on _____ Island.

2. Draw a line from each person who is talking to the words that person is saying.

3. Make a **D** on each person who is dizzy.

2 Write the name of each person the sentence tells about.

        Rosa   **Tony**   **Old Salt**

1. This person steered the boat most of the night.   _____

2. This person wanted the boat to be turned so that   _____
   it wouldn't make so much spray.

3. This person was the first one to spot Rose Island.   _____

4. This person climbed a tall tree.   _____

5. This person did not use a machete.   _____

6. This person found a real landmark.   _____

3 Write the words.

    under + brush = _____

    friend + ly   = _____

    land + mark = _____

    when + ever = _____

    spray + ing   = _____

1 Write the answers to these questions:

1. What color was everything inside the jungle? _____

2. When they had trouble finding another landmark, what did Salt think may have happened?

   _____

   _____

3. While they were resting, what scared Tony? _____

4. Tony looked for something to sit on. What did he see that was important?

   _____

5. Why were Tony and Rosa so happy at the end of this story?

   _____

   _____

2 Read the sentence and answer the questions.

Tony walked to the roots of the old tree and took out his compass in order to read the map.

1. Where did Tony walk? _____

2. Why did he take out his compass? _____

3. What kind of tree did Tony walk to? _____

3 The words in the first column have endings. Write the same words without endings in the second column.

landed _____

slipping _____

topped _____

pacing _____

sharing _____

4 Write the word **weather.** Make a line under **ea.** _____

Write the word **reflection.** Circle **tion.** _____

1 Look at the picture and do the items.

1. Circle the knife.
2. Make a box around the rocks that will come down the mountain.
3. Make an **X** on Tony.

2 Write the answers to these questions:

1. What did Tony find in the pile of rocks? _____

2. Where were Tony and Rosa when Salt pulled the rope that was tied to the knife handle?

   _____

3. What happened when the knife came out of the ground? _____

   _____

4. Where did Tony, Rosa, and Salt sleep that night?

   _____

5. What sounds could Tony hear just before he went to sleep?

   _____

3 Write the 2 words that make up each word.

sunlight   = _____ + _____

southwest = _____ + _____

landslide = _____ + _____

somehow = _____ + _____

become   = _____ + _____

1 Look at the picture and do the items.

1. Part of what people said is missing. Write the missing words in the blanks.
2. How did Salt know that they were digging in the wrong place?

2 Write **1, 2,** or **3** in front of each sentence to show when these things happened in the story. Then write the sentences in the blanks.

_____ **Salt said they were digging in the wrong place.**

_____ **Salt held up a gold coin.**

_____ **Everybody dug where the knife handle was.**

1. _____

2. _____

3. _____

3 Match the words and complete them.

garbage	ex
excited	le
beetle	tion
remove	gar
section	move

1 Write the name of the person each sentence tells about.
Salt   Tony

1. This person wedged the scoop of the shovel under the lid of the chest and pushed down. _____
2. This person thought that there would be red gems, gold drinking cups, and gold crowns in the chest. _____
3. This person thought one of the coins might be worth twenty dollars. _____
4. This person threw the shovel in the air and started dancing. _____

2 Read the sentence and answer the questions.
The third time Old Salt hit the rusty lock with his shovel, the lock fell to the ground in two pieces.

1. What kind of lock did Salt hit? _____
2. How many times did Salt have to hit the lock before it broke?
_____
3. What did Salt hit the lock with? _____
4. What happened when Salt hit the lock three times? _____
_____

3 The words in the first column have endings. Write the same words without endings in the second column.

shined   _____

gripped   _____

griped   _____

sobbing   _____

farmer   _____

4 Write the word **juice.** Make a line under **ce.**   _____

Write the word **hauled.** Circle **haul.**   _____

1 Look at the picture and do the items.

1. Draw a line from each person to the words that person is saying.
2. Draw a circle around the bags of gold.

2 Write the answers to these questions:
1. Which is easier—dragging the sacks or carrying them? _____
2. When Tony, Salt, and Rosa reached the top of the hill above the beach, how did they get
   the bags down? _____

   _____

3. What did they put on top of the gold in each sack?

   _____

4. How many sacks of gold were there? _____
5. How much money did Salt think the treasure was worth?

   _____

6. What did Salt say might take the treasure from them? _____

3 Write the words.

firm   +   er   =   _____

for   +   ever =   _____

rest   +   ed   =   _____

sun   +   set   =   _____

climb +   ing   =   _____

1 Write the answers to these questions:

1. What time of day did Tony, Rosa, and Salt agree to start back?

   _____

2. Why wouldn't they get much sleep if they tried to sleep near the boat?

   _____

3. When they started their trip back, how was the boat riding in the water?

   _____

4. How did the water change as the wind kept blowing?

   _____

5. Salt said that everybody would have to bail water from the boat to keep it from sinking. What did each person use to bail water?

   Rosa   _____

   Tony   _____

   Salt   _____

2 The words in the first column have endings. Write the same words without endings in the second column.

   firmer   _____

   fitted   _____

   slipping _____

   sloping   _____

   later   _____

3 Match the words and complete them.

   _____ sweat •   • all _____

   _____ squall •   • ge _____

   _____ fudge •   • in _____

   _____ supper •   • sw _____

   _____ invention •   • er _____

1 Look at the picture and do the items.

1. Put an **X** on the spot where Salt threw the first bag of gold.
2. Look at the bag in the box. Write the word **rocks** where you would find rocks and write the word **gold** where you would find gold.

3. Complete the arrow in front of the boat to show which way the nose of the boat will go after Salt moves some of the bags of gold.

2 Write the answers to these questions:

1. After Salt stopped singing, he talked about the sea. What did he say about the sea?

_____

_____

2. What things did Tony think about buying with his gold?

_____

_____

3. What problem was there at the end of this story?

_____

3 Write the 2 parts that make up each word.

maybe   = _____ + _____

hillside   = _____ + _____

nobody   = _____ + _____

throughout = _____ + _____

dotted   = _____ + _____

1 Use the code in Story 44 (on page 90) to figure out the secret message.

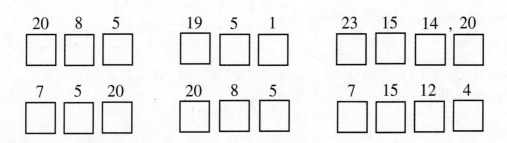

20 8 5   19 5 1   23 15 14 , 20

7 5 20   20 8 5   7 15 12 4

2 Write **1, 2,** or **3** in front of each sentence to show when these things happened in the story. Then write the sentences in the blanks.

_____ **Salt spotted Wake Island.**

_____ **Salt went to sleep behind the wheel of the truck.**

_____ **Salt, Rosa, and Tony transferred the gold from the boat to the truck.**

1. _____

_____

2. _____

_____

3. _____

_____

3 Match the words and complete them.

gentle   in

garbage   le

invitation   bage

circus   sp

spark   cus

LESSON 60

1 Write the name of the person each sentence tells about.

Mrs. Higgins   **Salt**   **Tony**

1. This person parked the truck in front of a no-parking zone at the airport. _____

2. This person wanted a cop to stand next to the truck. _____

3. This person couldn't move the truck from the no-parking zone. _____

4. This person was a customs officer. _____

5. This person wrote out a report about how the gold had been discovered. _____

6. This person ate eggs, toast, and lots of juice for breakfast—but not one banana. _____

7. Reporters liked to talk to this person the most. _____

2 The words in the first column have endings. Write the same words without endings in the second column.

sniper   _____

snipping   _____

filed   _____

teller   _____

climbing   _____

3 Write the words.

news   +   paper   = _____

dark   +   er   = _____

motor   +   boat   = _____

gentle   +   men   = _____

in   +   deed   = _____

4 Write the 1st sentence of Story 60.

_____

_____

1 Write the answers to these questions:

1. How many bags of gold did Salt, Tony, and Rosa bring back?

_____

2. Who really led Salt, Tony, and Rosa to the gold?

_____

3. What did Salt do with his eight bags of gold? _____

_____

4. Salt said he kept the treasure for himself. What was the real treasure?

_____

2 Read the sentence and answer the questions.

The day after Salt and the others came home, Tony was reading accounts of the treasure hunt in the newspaper.

1. Who was reading the newspaper accounts? _____

2. When was he reading the newspaper accounts?

_____

3. Where did he read the accounts? _____

3 The words in the first column have endings. Write the same words without endings in the second column.

drifted _____

dotted _____

tired _____

grins _____

dragging _____

4 Write the word **juice.** Circle **ce.** _____

Write the word **disappeared.** Make a line over **appear.** _____

LESSON 62

1 Look at the picture and do the items.

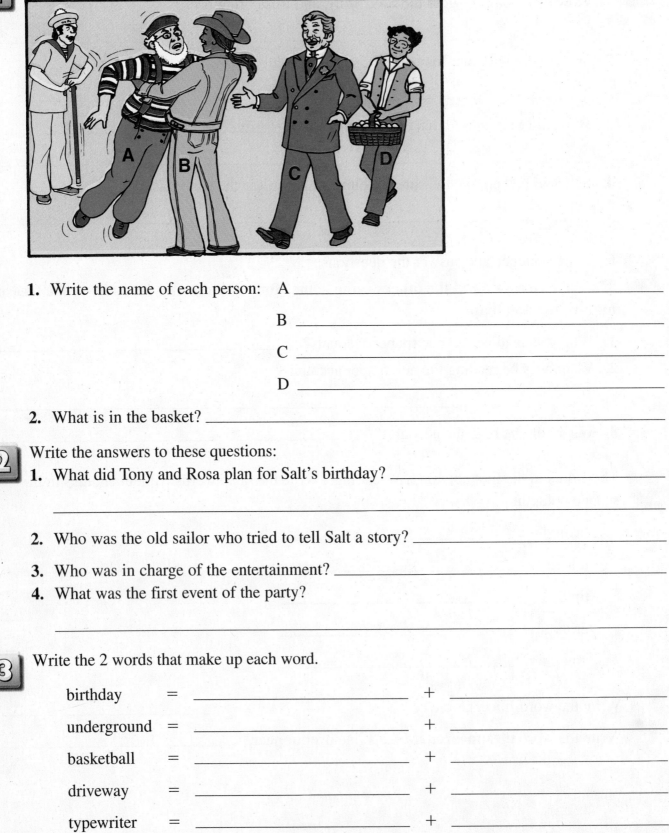

1. Write the name of each person: A _____

   B _____

   C _____

   D _____

2. What is in the basket? _____

2 Write the answers to these questions:

1. What did Tony and Rosa plan for Salt's birthday? _____

   _____

2. Who was the old sailor who tried to tell Salt a story? _____

3. Who was in charge of the entertainment? _____

4. What was the first event of the party?

   _____

3 Write the 2 words that make up each word.

   birthday   = _____ + _____

   underground   = _____ + _____

   basketball   = _____ + _____

   driveway   = _____ + _____

   typewriter   = _____ + _____

1 Look at the picture and do the items.

> YOU DIDN'T HAVE TO THROW A LINE DRIVE AT ME.
>
> LINE DRIVE, MY FOOT. IF YOU HAD PUT GLASSES ON, YOU MIGHT HAVE CAUGHT THAT EGG.
>
> A   B   C   D   E

Write the name of each person:

A _____   D _____

B _____   E _____

C _____

2 Write **1, 2,** or **3** in front of each sentence to show when these things happened in the story. Then write the sentences in the blanks.

_____ **Stan and Pete were thrown into the water.**

_____ **The con man passed out ostrich eggs.**

_____ **The president heaved a pie at the con man.**

1. _____

2. _____

3. _____

3 Match the words and complete them.

selection •   • ad

advice •   • ing

climbing •   • po

police •   • tch

batch •   • tion

LESSON 64

1 Write **1, 2,** or **3** in front of each sentence to show when these things happened in the story. Then write the sentences in the blanks.

_____ **Stan bid three chips and one shoe for a large box.**

_____ **The president spotted one person feeding pie to a dog under the table.**

_____ **The president gave Thin Jim a gold toothpick.**

1. _____

_____

2. _____

_____

3. _____

_____

2 Write the answers to these questions:

1. Who won the pie-eating contest? _____

2. What could people use to bid for things during the sale? _____

3. Why would Fuzz be able to bid a lot during the sale?

_____

4. What happened to Fuzz while he was telling about his jungle sickness?

_____

3 The words in the columns have endings. Write the same words without endings on the lines.

reporter _____   liking _____

slapped _____   walked _____

4 Write the words.

tooth + pick = _____

air + port = _____

over + looking = _____

sun + set = _____

motor + cycle = _____

1 Use the code in Story 44 (on page 91) to figure out the secret message.

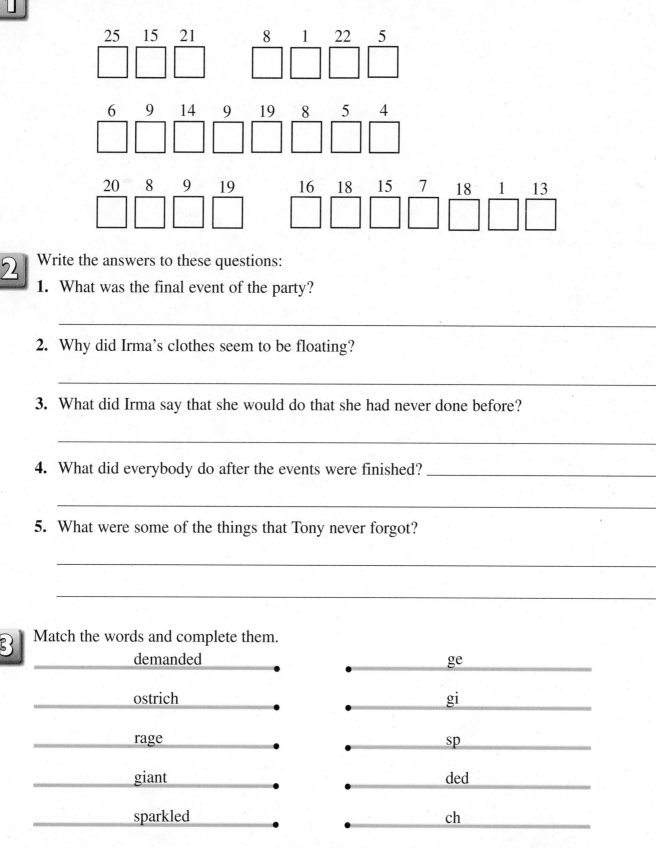

25 15 21   8 1 22 5
☐ ☐ ☐   ☐ ☐ ☐ ☐

6 9 14 9 19 8 5 4
☐ ☐ ☐ ☐ ☐ ☐ ☐ ☐

20 8 9 19   16 18 15 7 18 1 13
☐ ☐ ☐ ☐   ☐ ☐ ☐ ☐ ☐ ☐ ☐

2 Write the answers to these questions:

1. What was the final event of the party?

_____

2. Why did Irma's clothes seem to be floating?

_____

3. What did Irma say that she would do that she had never done before?

_____

4. What did everybody do after the events were finished? _____

_____

5. What were some of the things that Tony never forgot?

_____

_____

3 Match the words and complete them.

demanded   ge

ostrich   gi

rage   sp

giant   ded

sparkled   ch

Individual Reading Progress Chart
Decoding B2: LESSONS 2-35
LESSON NUMBER

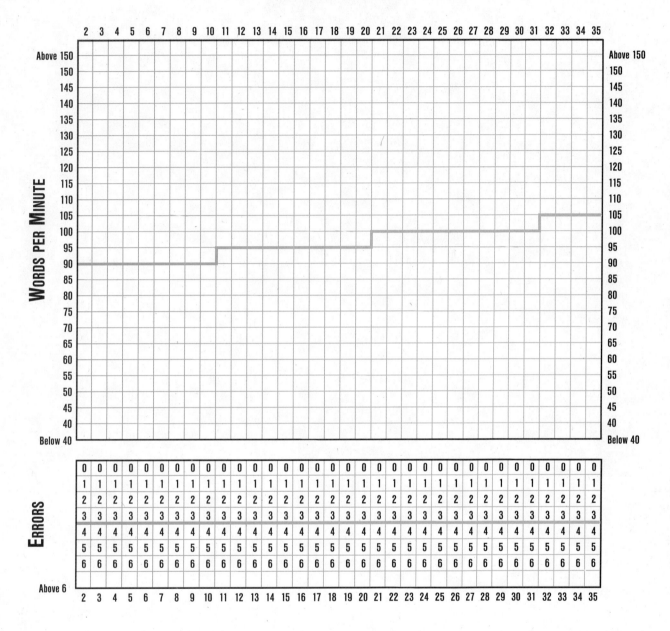

WORDS PER MINUTE

ERRORS

Individual Reading Progress Chart
Decoding B2: LESSONS 36-65

LESSON NUMBER

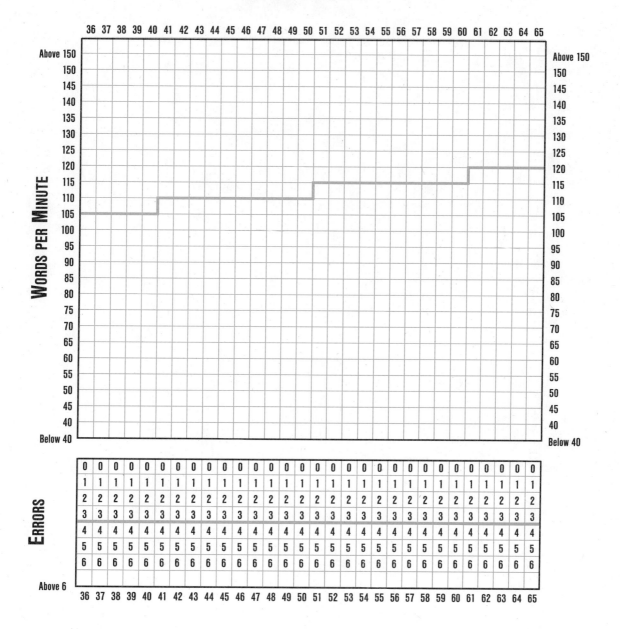